~A BINGO BOOK~

Ancient Egypt Bingo Book

COMPLETE BINGO GAME IN A BOOK

Tuthankamen's Burial Mask
Photo by Bjørn Christian Tørrissen

Written By Rebecca Stark

ISBN 978-0-87386-476-3

Educational Books 'n' Bingo

Printed in the U.S.A.

ANCIENT EGYPT BINGO DIRECTIONS

INCLUDED:

List of Terms

Templates for Additional Terms and Clues

2 Clues per Term

30 Unique Bingo Cards

Markers

1. **Either cut apart the book or make copies of ALL the sheets. You might want to make an extra copy of the clue sheets to use for introduction and review. Keep the sheets in an envelope for easy reuse.**

2. Cut apart the call cards with terms and clues.

3. Pass out one bingo card per student. There are enough for a class of 30.

4. Pass out markers. You may cut apart the markers included in this book or use any other small items of your choice.

5. Decide whether or not you will require the entire card to be filled. Requiring the entire card to be filled provides a better review. However, if you have a short time to fill, you may prefer to have them do the just the border or some other format. Tell the class before you begin what is required.

6. There are 50 terms. Read the list before you begin. If there are any terms that have not been covered in class, you may want to read to the students the term and clues before you begin.

7. There is a blank space in the middle of each card. You can instruct the students to use it as a free space or you can write in answers to cover terms not included. Of course, in this case you would create your own clues. (Templates provided.)

8. Shuffle the cards and place them in a pile. Two or three clues are provided for each term. If you plan to play the game with the same group more than once, you might want to choose a different clue for each game. If not, you may choose to use more than one clue.

9. Be sure to keep the cards you have used for the present game in a separate pile. When a student calls, "Bingo," he or she will have to verify that the correct answers are on his or her card AND that the markers were placed in response to the proper questions. Pull out the cards that are on the student's card keeping them in the order they were used in the game. Read each clue as it was given and ask the student to identify the correct answer from his or her card.

10. If the student has the correct answers on the card AND has shown that they were marked in response to the *correct questions,* then that student is the winner and the game is over. If the student does not have the correct answers on the card OR he or she marked the answers in response to *the wrong questions,* then the game continues until there is a proper winner.

11. If you want to play again, reshuffle the cards and begin again.

Have fun!

TERMS

ABU SIMBEL	NECROPOLIS
ALEXANDRIA	NEFERTITI
AKHENATEN	NEPHTHYS
AMON-RE	NILE RIVER
APIS	NUBIA
ARCHAEOLOGIST	NUN
ARTIFACT	NUT
BOOK OF THE DEAD	OBELISK
HOWARD CARTER	OSIRIS
CARTOUCHE	PAPYRUS
CLEOPATRA	PHARAOH
ENNEAD	PYRAMIDS
GEB	RA
GIZA	RAMESSES II
HATHOR	ROSETTA STONE
HATSHEPSUT	SCARAB
HIEROGLYPHICS	SET (SETH)
HORUS	SETI I
IMHOTEP	SHU
IRRIGATION	SPHINX
ISIS	TEFNUT
KA	THEBES
MAAT	THOTH
MEMPHIS	THUTMOSE III
MUMMIFICATION	TUTANKHAMEN

Additional Terms

Choose as many additional erms as you would like and write them in the squares. Repeat each as desired.
Cut out the squares and randomly distribute them to the class.
Instruct the students to place their square on the center space of their card.

Ancient Egypt Bingo

Clues for
Additional Terms

Write three clues for each of your additional terms.

_____ 1. 2. 3.	_____ 1. 2. 3.
_____ 1. 2. 3.	_____ 1. 2. 3.
_____ 1. 2. 3.	_____ 1. 2. 3.

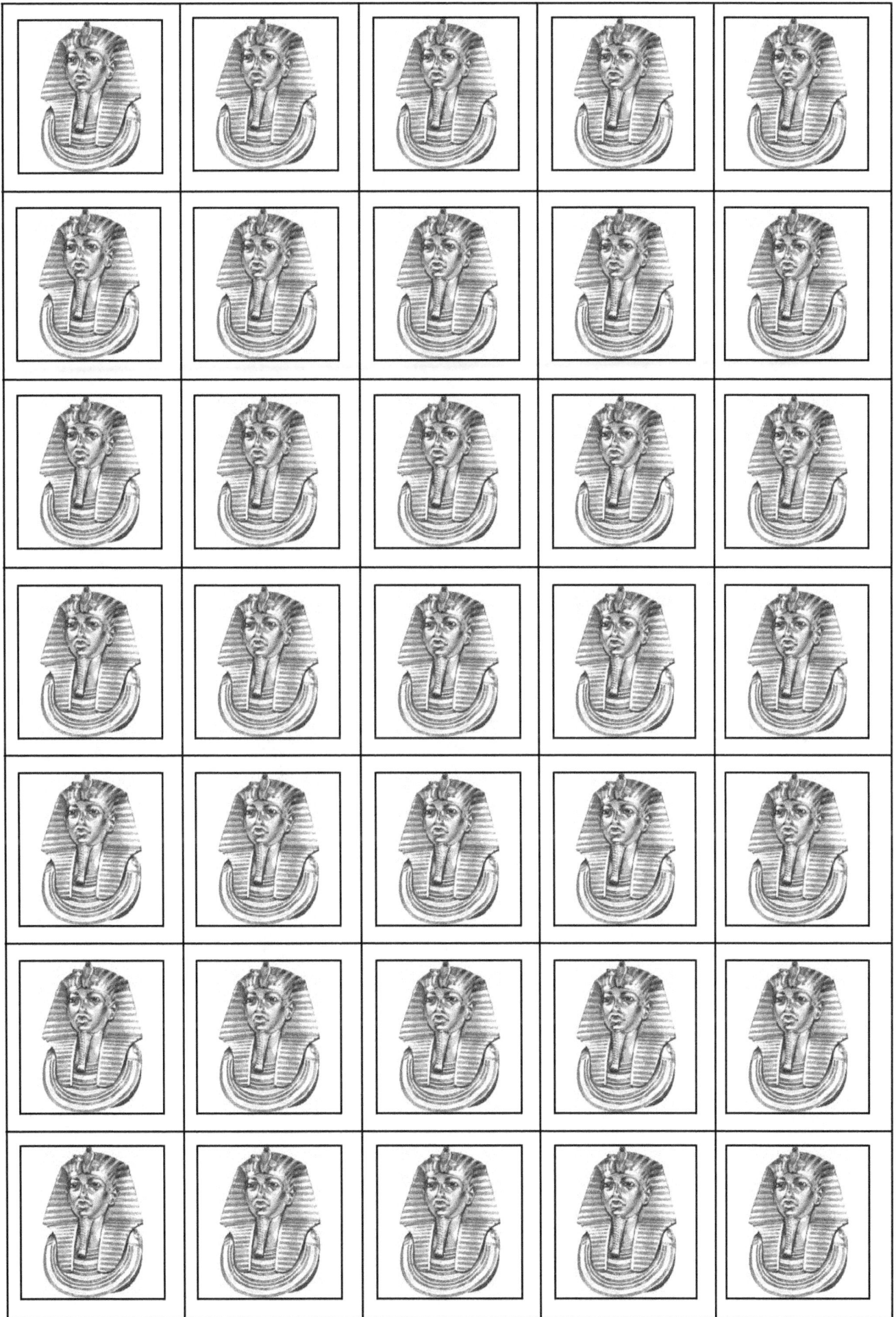

ABU SIMBEL
1. The site comprises 2 massive rock temples in southern Egypt.
2. Ramesses II built the temples here as a lasting monument to himself and to his queen Nefertari.
3. In modern times the 2 temples here were relocated to avoid being submerged during the creation of Lake Nasser.

ALEXANDRIA
1. It was the capital of Egypt from 332 BCE to 641 CE.
2. It was founded c. 331 BCE by the Greek Macedonian king Alexander the Great.
3. The lighthouse here was considered one of the Seven Ancient Wonders.

AKHENATEN
1. He was first known as Amenhotep IV.
2. He tried to get the Egyptians to change to the monotheistic worship of Aten.
3. His chief wife was Nefertiti.

AMON-RE
1. Originally, this god was known only as Amon, or Amen and sometimes Amun.
2. He is sometimes called "the king of the Egyptian gods."
3. Two deities were combined during the New Kingdom, resulting in this god.

APIS
1. This bull-deity was worshiped in Memphis.
2. It was the most important of all the sacred animals in Egypt.
3. This bull had to have a white triangle on its forehead, the outline of a white vulture wing on its back, a scarab mark under its tongue, a white crescent moon shape on its right flank, and double hairs on its tail.

ARCHAEOLOGIST
1. This kind of scientist studies people and what they did from the things they left behind.
2. This kind of scientist looks for artifacts from past civilizations.
3. Howard Carter was one; he discovered the tomb of Tutankhamen.

ARTIFACT
1. It is any object made or modified by a human culture.
2. Sometimes the word is used to refer only to simple, hand-made objects representative of a particular culture.
3. Many fascinating ones from Tutankhamen's tomb have been exhibited in museums.

BOOK OF THE DEAD
1. This is the name often given to the ancient Egyptian funerary text.
2. This funerary text provides a description of the ancient Egyptian conception of the afterlife.
3. This text provides a collection of hymns, spells, and instructions to allow the deceased to pass through obstacles in the afterlife.

HOWARD CARTER
1. This archaeologist discovered Tutankhamen's tomb.
2. In addition to finding Tutankhamen's tomb, he found the remains of Queen Hatshepsut's tomb in Deir el-Bahri.
3. Lord Carnarvon financed this archaeologist's search for the tomb of a previously unknown pharaoh, Tutankhamen.

Ancient Egypt Bingo

CARTOUCHE
1. This is an oblong enclosure with a horizontal line at one end; the hieroglyphic text enclosed was a royal name.
2. These helped translators decipher the hieroglyphic writing on the Rosetta Stone because they knew they enclosed royal names.
3. Amulets in this form were placed in tombs to display the name of the king buried there.

CLEOPATRA

1. She shared her power with her father Ptolemy XII and later with her brothers/husbands Ptolemy XIII and Ptolemy XIV.
2. She had four children, one by Julius Caesar, named Caesarion, and three by Mark Antony.
3. She committed suicide in 30 BCE, allegedly by means of an asp bite.

ENNEAD

1. A grouping of 9 deities.
2. The most important one included Atum; Atum's children Shu and Tefnut; and their descendants Geb, Isis, Nephthys, Nut, Osiris, and Set.
3. Some pharaohs created an ___ that included themselves; for example, Seti I worshipped one that combined 6 important deities with 3 deified forms of himself.

GEB

1. He was the personification of the earth in the grouping of 9 deities known as the Great Ennead.
2. In the Great Ennead, he is the husband of Nut and the son of Tefnut and Shu.
3. In the Great Ennead he was the father of the 4 lesser gods in that ennead: Osiris, Set, Isis and Nephthys.

GIZA

1. Sir Flinders Petrie's 1880–82 survey of the this plateau included the Great Pyramid of Khufu.
2. This plateau is the site of many impressive ancient monuments, including the Great Sphinx and the Great Pyramid.
3. The Great Pyramid here is also known as Khufu's Pyramid.

HATHOR

1. This ancient goddess was worshiped as a cow-deity during the Second Dynasty.
2. She was originally a personification of the Milky Way, which was depicted as the milk that flowed from the udders of a heavenly cow.
3. One aspect of this goddess was Sekhmet, the Eye of Ra.

HATSHEPSUT

1. She was the fifth pharaoh of the Eighteenth Dynasty and had a long and successful reign.
.2. She reigned longer than any other woman of an Egyptian dynasty.
3. She was the elder daughter of Thutmose I and Queen Ahmose and was the successor to Thutmose II.

HIEROGLYPHICS

1. In this formal writing system pictorial symbols were used to represent meanings or sounds or a combination of meaning and sound.
2. Egyptians used a cursive form for religious literature on papyrus and wood.
3. As writing developed, simplified forms of this kind of writing developed, resulting in hieratic, or priestly, and demotic, or popular, scripts.

HORUS

1. This god was depicted with a man's body and a falcon's head.
2. It was said that the sun was one of his eyes and the moon the other, and that they crossed the sky when he flew across it as a falcon.
3. It was said that the moon is not as bright as the sun because this god lost the eye representing the moon in a battle with Set.

IMHOTEP

1. ___ designed the Pyramid of Djoser at Saqqara and may have been responsible for the first known use of columns in architecture.
2. This architect/engineer was one of a few commoners to be accorded divine status after death. It is believed that his tomb is at Saqqara.
3. He was not only an architect and engineer, but also the founder of Egyptian medicine.

IRRIGATION

1. It is the artificial application of water to the soil, usually for assisting in growing crops.
2. Early attempts at this were made through the use of canals to flood large tracts of land while the Nile was flowing high.
3. The design of this kind of system in the Nile Valley depended on knowing in advance the height of the annual flood.

ISIS
1. This goddess was thought to be the ideal mother and wife. Her name literally means "queen of the throne."
2. She was mother of Horus and wife and sister of Osiris.
3. According to one myth, this goddess tricked Re into revealing his secret name and thereby obtained many magical powers.

KA
1. Ancient Egyptians believed that death occurs when this life force leaves the body.
2. One of the five parts of the soul.
3. Ancient Egyptians believed that the Ba, or personality, was united with this in the afterlife.

MAAT
1. Sometimes personified as a goddess, this was the ancient Egyptian concept of truth and order.
2. She weighed souls in the underworld.
3. Her feather determined whether or not the souls of the departed would reach the afterlife successfully.

MEMPHIS
1. During the Old Kingdom, this city served as the nation's capital and it was the location of the kings' primary residence.
2. This ancient capital was founded by Menes soon after the unification of Egypt.
3. Two necropoleis, Saqqara and Giza, were very near this city.

MUMMIFICATION
1. Because eternal life was important to the ancient Egyptians, they practiced this process to preserve the body forever.
2. This process was improved when embalmers learned to use natural salts to remove moisture from the body.
3. During this process all organs except the heart were removed and stored in canopic jars.

NECROPOLIS
1. This is the name for a large elaborate cemetery of an ancient city.
2. Saqqara is the oldest one of unified Egypt.
3. This is a Greek word meaning "city of the dead."

NEFERTITI
1. Known for her beauty, she was the chief wife of the Pharaoh Akhenaten.
2. She and her husband Akhenaten were known for trying to change Egypt's religion.
3. Her name means "the beautiful one has arrived."

NEPHTHYS
1. In the Great Ennead, she was a daughter of Nut and Geb and a sister of Osiris, Isis and Set.
2. She was usually portrayed as a woman wearing the symbol of her name on her head or on top of a pair of horns.
3. Nebt-het, the correct transliteration of her name, means "lady of the house." "House" referred to the portion of the sky where Horus lived.

NILE RIVER
1. Along with water and fertile soil, it provided transportation and enabled the Egyptians to interact with other civilizations
2. In about 3000 BCE settlements began to appear in the small fertile area around it.
3. Its floods allowed Egyptian farmers to grow crops such as dates, figs, and pomegranates.

NUBIA
1. This is the name for the region in southern Egypt in what is now northern Sudan.
2. Kush civilization, one of the earliest civilizations to develop in the Nile River Valley, was centered this region.
3. This area of the Nile Valley was home to three Kushite kingdoms; they were centered in Kerma, Napata, and Meroë.

NUN 1. In the mythology of ancient Egypt, this is the name of the primordial waters from which the creator god sprang. 2. More than an ocean, he was a limitless expanse of motionless water. 3. He was portrayed as a blue- or green-bearded man, symbolizing water and fertility. He held a palm frond, a symbol of long life.	**NUT** 1. This goddess of the Great Ennead was the personification of the sky and of the heavens and the daughter of Shu and Tefnut. 2. She is often shown with her hands and feet touching the ground so that her body forms a semi-circle to represent the heavens. 2. According to one myth she gave birth to her son the sun-god daily.
OBELISK 1. These tall, narrow, four-sided monuments taper and end in a pyramidal top. 2. These monuments were prominent in the architecture of the ancient Egyptians; they often placed them in pairs at the entrance of temples. 3. Ancient ones were monoliths; in other words, they were made from one stone.	**OSIRIS** 1. After being killed by Set, he could no longer dwell in the land of the living, so he lived in the underworld as the lord of the dead. 2. At the height of Egyptian civilization, he was the primary deity and second only to his father, Ra, in power. 3. According to one legend, after Set killed him, Isis briefly brought him back to life.
PAPYRUS 1. This is a thick paper-like material produced from soft center of the stems of a plant by the same name. 2. The plant used to make this paper-like material was once abundant in the Nile Delta. 3. The ancient Egyptians used this plant for boats, mattresses and mats as well as for paper.	**PHARAOH** 1. This is the name for a religious/political leader in the New Kingdom of ancient Egypt. 2. The name means "Great House" and it originally referred to the king's palace. 3. Although most were male, the same title was used when a female ruled.
PYRAMIDS 1. These huge structures were built as tombs for the pharaohs during the Old and Middle Kingdoms. 2. Three famous ones are those of Khufu, Khafre and Menkaure. 3. The oldest and largest is the one built for the fourth-dynasty pharaoh Khufu; it remained the largest man-made structure for over 3,800 years.	**RA** 1. The central god of the Egyptian pantheon, this sun-god later combined with Amon. 2. Pharaohs were considered his children. 3. This sun-god appeared as a pharaoh wearing the sun disk on his head.
RAMESSES II 1. The third pharaoh of the Nineteenth Dynasty, he is often regarded as Egypt's greatest and most powerful pharaoh. 2. Among his many building accomplishments were the two temples at Abu Simbel and the hypostyle hall at Karnak. 3. He built the Ramesseum, his great mortuary temple, on the site of Seti I's ruined temple. Ancient Egypt Bingo	**ROSETTA STONE** 1. The text on this stele is made up of 3 translations of a single passage: hieroglyphic, demotic, and classical Greek. 2. Its translation by Thomas Young and François Champollion contributed to the decipherment of the principles of hieroglyphic writing. 3. The text of this stele is a decree from Ptolemy V. **© Barbara M. Peller**

SCARAB 1. This is an amulet in the shape of a dung beetle used in ancient Egypt as a talisman. 2. This is the name given to the dung beetle worshiped by the ancient Egyptians as an embodiment of the god Khepri. 3. The opening and closing of this beetle's colorful wings symbolized night and day.	**SET (SETH)** 1. Brother of Isis, Nephthys, and Osiris, this god of the Great Ennead was originally the god of the desert, storms, and chaos. 2. He killed his older brother Osiris in an attempt to gain the throne. 3. This god of the Ennead was sometimes depicted as a man with the head of an unknown animal.
SETI I 1. This pharaoh was the father one of Egypt's greatest rulers, Ramesses II. 2. This pharaoh is responsible for beginning the Hypostyle Hall in the Temple of Amen at Karnak. It was completed by his son, Ramesses II. 3. His tomb, one of the finest in the Valley of the Kings, was discovered a few days after that of his father, Ramesses I.	**SHU** 1. This god of the Great Ennead was a personification of air. 2. This god of the Great Ennead was created by Atum from his breath. 3. This god is often depicted holding up his daughter Nut, the sky goddess, over his son Geb, the Earth, separating the two.
SPHINX 1. This monument is a half-human, half-lion statue on the Giza Plateau. 2. This is the largest monolith statue in the world and the earliest known monumental statue. 3. Many Egyptologists think this half-human, half-lion statue represents the likeness of King Khafra.	**TEFNUT** 1. A goddess of the Great Ennead, she is goddess of water and fertility; her name means "moist waters." 2. According to 1 legend, she was upset with her father and fled into Nubia, taking the water & moisture with her and causing Egypt to dry up. 3. One myth says her father, Ra, sent Thoth and Shu to get her back after she ran away to Nubia.
THEBES 1. The modern-day city of Luxor is at the site of this ancient Egyptian city. 2. Several great monuments were located there: the Ramesseum, mortuary temple of Ramesses II; Medinet Habu, the temple of Ramses III; and the temple of the female pharaoh Hatshepsut. 3. The Valley of the Kings was on the west bank of the Nile, across from this city.	**THOTH** 1. This god was often shown as a man with the head of an Ibis. Sometimes he was depicted as an ibis or as a baboon. 2. After Isis gathered the pieces of Osiris's dismembered body, this god gave her the words to resurrect him. 3. This god of writing and wisdom was also associated with the moon.
THUTMOSE III (THUTMOSIS III) 1. During the first 22 years of his 54-year reign this pharaoh was co-regent with his stepmother, Hatshepsut. 2. This pharaoh was responsible for building over 50 temples and for the massive additions to the temple at Karnak. 3. His son Amenhotep II succeeded this pharaoh. Ancient Egypt Bingo	**TUTANKHAMEN (TUTANKHAMUN)** 1. His name contains a word that means "life." That same word is the name of a very important amulet used in ancient Egypt to signify life. 2. The 1922 discovery of his intact tomb by Howard Carter sparked a renewed interest in ancient Egypt. 3. He was 8 or 9 years old when he became pharaoh and he reigned for about 10 years. **© Barbara M. Peller**

Ancient Egypt Bingo

Imhotep	Abu Simbel	Artifact	Alexandria	Nubia
The Book of the Dead	Akhenaten	Thebes	Nut	Thoth
Amon-Re	Tutankhamen		Giza	Cleopatra
Pyramids	Horus	Thutmose III	Nefertiti	Papyrus
Scarab	Ra	Set (Seth)	Tefnut	Sphinx

Ancient Egypt Bingo

Pyramids	Amon-Re	Nun	Obelisk	Mummification
Papyrus	Hathor	Apis	Howard Carter	Nephthys
Geb	Ka		Irrigation	Thutmose III
Scarab	Pharaoh	Tutankhamen	The Rosetta Stone	Sphinx
Thoth	Thebes	Set (Seth)	The Book of the Dead	Tefnut

Ancient Egypt Bingo

Pyramids	Thutmose III	Hathor	Nefertiti	Amon-Re
Nut	Akhenaten	Ennead	Abu Simbel	Howard Carter
Horus	Thebes		Nephthys	Archaeologist
Tutankhamen	Geb	Shu	Ra	Nun
Tefnut	The Book of the Dead	Set (Seth)	The Rosetta Stone	Mummification

Ancient Egypt Bingo

Tutankhamen	Nephthys	Artifact	Howard Carter	Mummification
The Nile River	Cartouche	Abu Simbel	Ra	Amon-Re
Giza	Scarab		Nubia	Alexandria
Thutmose III	Hatshepsut	Thebes	Set (Seth)	Apis
Howard Carter	Thoth	Pharaoh	Tefnut	Cleopatra

Ancient Egypt Bingo: Card No. 4

Ancient Egypt Bingo

Thoth	Nubia	Horus	Ka	The Book of the Dead
The Nile River	Thutmose III	Ennead	Irrigation	Akhenaten
Ra	Cleopatra		Nut	Maat
Sphinx	Mummification	Imhotep	The Rosetta Stone	Hatshepsut
Hathor	Set (Seth)	Amon-Re	Tutankhamen	Giza

Ancient Egypt Bingo: Card No. 5

© Barbara M. Peller

Ancient Egypt Bingo

Archaeologist	Nephthys	Nun	Mummification	Cleopatra
Nefertiti	Horus	Hieroglyphics	Abu Simbel	Amon-Re
Obelisk	Howard Carter		Cartouche	Irrigation
Set (Seth)	Sphinx	The Rosetta Stone	Pharaoh	Artifact
Papyrus	Apis	Imhotep	Giza	Hatshepsut

© Barbara M. Peller

Ancient Egypt Bingo

Imhotep	Nephthys	Maat	Nut	Hathor
Papyrus	Mummification	Ka	Akhenaten	The Nile River
Nun	Alexandria		Irrigation	Ra
Tutankhamen	Scarab	Ennead	Pyramids	Geb
Set (Seth)	The Book of the Dead	The Rosetta Stone	Pharaoh	Archaeologist

Ancient Egypt Bingo

Ancient Egypt Bingo

Giza	Nephthys	Isis	Nefertiti	Cartouche
The Nile River	Artifact	Obelisk	Cleopatra	Apis
Hatshepsut	Ramesses II		Mummification	Nubia
Tefnut	Tutankhamen	Pyramids	Howard Carter	Scarab
Thebes	Set (Seth)	Pharaoh	Horus	Papyrus

Ancient Egypt Bingo

Irrigation	Hathor	Ka	Hatshepsut	The Book of the Dead
Ra	Mummification	Geb	Horus	Giza
Necropolis	Imhotep		Akhenaten	Isis
Hieroglyphics	Sphinx	Ramesses II	Nut	Maat
Scarab	The Rosetta Stone	Ennead	Pyramids	Nubia

© Barbara M. Peller

Ancient Egypt Bingo

Pyramids	Nefertiti	Cartouche	Obelisk	Hieroglyphics
Cleopatra	Apis	Abu Simbel	Akhenaten	Mummification
Ramesses II	Nephthys		Alexandria	Geb
Set (Seth)	Sphinx	Hatshepsut	The Rosetta Stone	Necropolis
Ennead	Papyrus	Nun	Thoth	Giza

Ancient Egypt Bingo

Archaeologist	Nephthys	Horus	Hatshepsut	Papyrus
Isis	Necropolis	Nut	Irrigation	Abu Simbel
The Nile River	Mummification		Nun	Ka
Ennead	Shu	The Rosetta Stone	The Book of the Dead	Pyramids
Howard Carter	Set (Seth)	Ra	Pharaoh	Hathor

Ancient Egypt Bingo

Hathor	Nubia	Necropolis	Nefertiti	Irrigation
Ka	Papyrus	Artifact	Pharaoh	Akhenaten
Imhotep	Maat		Cleopatra	Obelisk
Set (Seth)	Scarab	Mummification	Pyramids	The Nile River
Nephthys	Isis	Ramesses II	Howard Carter	Apis

Ancient Egypt Bingo

Hatshepsut	Nubia	Archaeologist	Necropolis	Cleopatra
Artifact	Isis	Mummification	Irrigation	Geb
Nefertiti	Hathor		Ka	Maat
Giza	The Rosetta Stone	Cartouche	Ramesses II	Pyramids
Set (Seth)	Ra	Pharaoh	Imhotep	Nut

Ancient Egypt Bingo

The Book of the Dead	Mummification	Horus	Irrigation	Howard Carter
Apis	Imhotep	Necropolis	Akhenaten	Nephthys
Hieroglyphics	Alexandria		Nun	Ennead
Sphinx	The Rosetta Stone	Ramesses II	Cartouche	Archaeologist
Set (Seth)	Obelisk	Geb	Papyrus	Giza

Ancient Egypt Bingo

Nut	Ra	Horus	Hathor	Nefertiti
Archaeologist	Nun	Abu Simbel	Artifact	Howard Carter
Cleopatra	Imhotep		Amon-Re	Nephthys
Set (Seth)	Necropolis	Isis	The Rosetta Stone	Hieroglyphics
Papyrus	Scarab	Pharaoh	Hatshepsut	Ka

Ancient Egypt Bingo

Cartouche	Necropolis	Isis	Hatshepsut	Howard Carter
Obelisk	Geb	Maat	The Nile River	Alexandria
Hieroglyphics	Nubia		Cleopatra	Ka
Tutankhamen	Apis	Set (Seth)	Osiris	Pyramids
Shu	Seti I	Pharaoh	Scarab	Nephthys

Ancient Egypt Bingo

Ennead	Osiris	Ra	Necropolis	The Book of the Dead
Nut	Howard Carter	The Rosetta Stone	Alexandria	Maat
Irrigation	Giza		Seti I	Isis
Sphinx	Papyrus	Pyramids	Horus	Geb
Shu	Hatshepsut	Hathor	Nefertiti	Nubia

Ancient Egypt Bingo

Hatshepsut	Ramesses II	Apis	Hieroglyphics	Obelisk
Nephthys	Ennead	Ka	Cleopatra	Howard Carter
Irrigation	Geb		Memphis	Artifact
Sphinx	Abu Simbel	The Rosetta Stone	Pyramids	Nun
Seti I	Necropolis	Horus	Archaeologist	Osiris

Ancient Egypt Bingo

Cleopatra	Ra	Necropolis	Isis	Cleopatra
Nut	Nefertiti	Nephthys	Hathor	Alexandria
Osiris	The Book of the Dead		Akhenaten	Amon-Re
Nun	Seti I	The Rosetta Stone	Scarab	Memphis
Artifact	Shu	Papyrus	Giza	Pharaoh

Ancient Egypt
Bingo

Ancient Egypt Bingo

Ramesses II	Osiris	Nefertiti	Necropolis	Pharaoh
Apis	Ka	The Nile River	Howard Carter	Obelisk
Nubia	Maat		Tutankhamen	Abu Simbel
Thoth	Thebes	Tefnut	Scarab	Seti I
Thutmose III	Giza	Shu	Pyramids	Memphis

Ancient Egypt Bingo

Nut	Archaeologist	The Nile River	Necropolis	Thoth
Nubia	Memphis	Cartouche	Isis	Imhotep
Geb	Papyrus		Osiris	Horus
Tefnut	Hathor	Seti I	Sphinx	Giza
Tutankhamen	Shu	Pharaoh	Ennead	Scarab

Ancient Egypt Bingo

Hatshepsut	Nun	Memphis	Artifact	Hieroglyphics
Obelisk	Nefertiti	Amon-Re	Isis	Akhenaten
Apis	Alexandria		Imhotep	Maat
Seti I	Sphinx	Ra	Abu Simbel	The Book of the Dead
Shu	Ennead	Osiris	Geb	The Nile River

Ancient Egypt Bingo

Cartouche	Osiris	Hathor	Artifact	Pharaoh
Archaeologist	Ramesses II	Papyrus	Nut	Abu Simbel
Nun	Hieroglyphics		Tefnut	Imhotep
Geb	Shu	Ra	Ennead	Scarab
Thoth	Thebes	Giza	Tutankhamen	Memphis

Ancient Egypt Bingo

Cartouche	Ramesses II	The Book of the Dead	Osiris	Isis
Memphis	Pharaoh	The Nile River	Obelisk	Imhotep
Maat	Hatshepsut		Hieroglyphics	Geb
Thoth	Tefnut	Seti I	Ennead	Nubia
Thutmose III	Tutankhamen	Shu	Nefertiti	Thebes

Ancient Egypt Bingo

Tutankhamen	The Nile River	Osiris	Horus	Memphis
Abu Simbel	Sphinx	Nut	Cartouche	Akhenaten
Nubia	Isis		Tefnut	Seti I
Amon-Re	Thoth	Thebes	Shu	Alexandria
Pharaoh	The Book of the Dead	Apis	Howard Carter	Thutmose III

Ancient Egypt Bingo

Memphis	Osiris	Nun	Obelisk	Hieroglyphics
Apis	Nefertiti	Isis	Ramesses II	Cartouche
Sphinx	Tefnut		Alexandria	Tutankhamen
Ennead	Artifact	Thoth	Shu	Seti I
Maat	Howard Carter	Horus	Thebes	Thutmose III

Ancient Egypt Bingo

Nun	Apis	Osiris	Ramesses II	Ka
Thoth	Tefnut	Nut	Seti I	Akhenaten
The Rosetta Stone	Thebes		Shu	Tutankhamen
Hieroglyphics	Archaeologist	The Nile River	Thutmose III	Abu Simbel
Howard Carter	Alexandria	Memphis	Amon-Re	Maat

Ancient Egypt Bingo

Cleopatra	Ramesses II	Amon-Re	Osiris	Cartouche
Ka	Memphis	Tefnut	Obelisk	Alexandria
Thebes	Geb		Maat	Nubia
Pyramids	Hieroglyphics	Papyrus	Shu	Seti I
Artifact	Irrigation	Howard Carter	Thutmose III	Thoth

Ancient Egypt Bingo

Memphis	Ramesses II	Hieroglyphics	Nut	Irrigation
Sphinx	Cleopatra	The Nile River	Maat	Amon-Re
Nubia	Tefnut		Akhenaten	Osiris
Horus	Thoth	Mummification	Shu	Seti I
Howard Carter	Isis	Thutmose III	Archaeologist	Thebes

Ancient Egypt Bingo

The Book of the Dead	Osiris	Obelisk	Irrigation	Seti I
Abu Simbel	Ramesses II	Nun	Alexandria	Akhenaten
Sphinx	Hieroglyphics		Maat	The Nile River
Thutmose III	Archaeologist	Artifact	Shu	Tefnut
Thoth	Hathor	Thebes	Memphis	Amon-Re

www.ingramcontent.com/pod-product-compliance
Lightning Source LLC
LaVergne TN
LVHW061336060426
835511LV00014B/1959